First World War
and Army of Occupation
War Diary
France, Belgium and Germany

58 DIVISION
Headquarters, Branches and Services
Royal Army Medical Corps
Assistant Director Medical Services
1 October 1915 - 22 February 1916

WO95/2993/1

Published by

The Naval & Military Press Ltd

Unit 10 Ridgewood Industrial Park,

Uckfield, East Sussex,

TN22 5QE England

Tel: +44 (0) 1825 749494

www.naval-military-press.com

www.nmarchive.com

This diary has been reprinted in facsimile from the original. Any imperfections are inevitably reproduced and the quality may fall short of modern type and cartographic standards.

© Crown Copyright
Images reproduced by permission of The National Archives, London, England, 2015.

Contents

Document type	Place/Title	Date From	Date To
Heading	WO95/2993/1		
Heading	58 Division (2/1 London Div) A.D.M.S. 1915 Oct-1916 Feb		
Miscellaneous	War Diary Statement for August, 1915.	03/09/1915	03/09/1915
War Diary	Ipswich	01/10/1915	25/10/1915
War Diary	Ipswich	02/11/1915	17/12/1915
War Diary	Ipswich	14/01/1916	31/01/1916
War Diary	Ipswich	21/02/1916	22/02/1916

WO 95/2993/1

58 DIVISION
(2/1 LONDON DIV)

A.D.M.S

1915 OCT – 1916 FEB

WAR DIARY STATEMENT

for
August, 1915.

UNIT.   R.A.M.C.

DIVISION.   58th (London) Division.

MOBILIZATION CENTRE.   London.

STATIONS SINCE OCCUPIED.   Bisley, Crowborough, Ipswich.

TRAINING.   Progress satisfactory. Lectures by Major Barry very good and much appreciated. Field Training with Brigadier very useful.

DISCIPLINE.   Good - a few minor offences.

ADMINISTRATION.

Veterinary services - Satisfactory.

Supply   "   "

Ordnance   "   "

Billeting   "   "

Channels of correspondence - Satisfactory.

Supply of remounts - Still short.

REORGANIZATION INTO HOME AND IMPERIAL SERVICES.   Completed.

PREPARATION FOR IMPERIAL SERVICE.   With the exception of a shortage in officers and special departments such as "dispensers", all units are approaching fitness. Each unit has a considerable number of recruits undertraining. They are mostly very intelligent men and quickly pick up the work.

GENERAL REMARKS.

The shortage of Medical Officers, especially in the Field Ambulances, is still very serious, and it seems almost impossible to obtain them.

COLONEL,
Assistant Director Medical Services,
58th (London) DIVISION.

Red House Park,
Ipswich,
3rd September, 1915.

Army Form C. 2118.

WAR DIARY
INTELLIGENCE SUMMARY.
(Erase heading not required.)

Instructions regarding War Diaries and Intelligence Summaries are contained in F.S. Regs., Part II. and the Staff Manual respectively. Title pages will be prepared in manuscript.

Hour, Date, Place	Summary of Events and Information	Remarks and references to Appendices
Ipswich Oct 1915		
Oct. 1.	A.D.M.S. proceeded on short leave of absence	
8.	Inspection of camping ground of Heavy By. R.G.A. Gave advice re disposal of manure who re. slunkel. Recruit M.O. & men. Arranged for med' attendance on unit, & leaving no M.O.	
11.	Attended exhibition of Splint, & dressings when if wound treatment at medical Society London. Gather into ar wowing M.O. & B division as could be spared. A.D.M.S granted leave on med certificate for 3 weeks	
13.	Inspected a draft of 47 men of 2 Lond. Fd. Co. R.E. at Needham market for service overseas — a few months chaft one man, unvaccinated reinoculated was rejected by a working men.	
16.	Ext 2/3 Lond Fd. Ambulance at Woodbridge — recommend control et 6	
3.	Shed gave advice regarding Road. Also inspected troops at 6 toffees servings	

C. G. [signature]
Lieut. Col. A.D.M.S. for
D. A. D. M. S.,
COLONEL Medical Services,
Assistant Director Medical Services
58th (London) DIVISION.

WAR DIARY
INTELLIGENCE SUMMARY.
(Erase heading not required.)

Army Form C. 2118.

Hour, Date, Place	Summary of Events and Information	Remarks and references to Appendices
Oct 19.	D.D.M.S. Central Force inspected Warren Heath Camp. Complained of the state of the kitchens infested with flies & recommended measures for their removal which have not yet been successful. Large accumulation of stable manure occurred. I feel sure it has not yet been removed. This, in the opinion of the D.D.M.S. is the direct cause of the nuisance. The difficulty re stable manure exists in all stations where there are mounted troops.	
22.	Brigade field day in which the three field ambulances 378 took part + furnished spunk offered cuts.	
23.	Visited Framlingham with D.S.O. Advised individual 287 officer in interim posts. Consulted with O.C. Brigade concerning mud trenching over engineers.	
25.	Asst. D. 1st Army visited Ipswich; discussed army matters for discharge on A.F.B. 204.	

G. F. Gubbins
Lieut. Col. D.A.D.M.S. for
COLONEL.
Assistant Director Medical Services,
58th (London) DIVISION.

WAR DIARY
or
INTELLIGENCE SUMMARY.
(Erase heading not required.)

Army Form C. 2118.

Stamp: -8 DEC 1915 REGISTRY, FIRST ARMY, CENTRAL FORCE
Stamp: A.D.M.S. 58th (LONDON) DIVISION, No. M.184

Hour, Date, Place	Summary of Events and Information	Remarks and references to Appendices
Ipswich 2-11-15	1st Infantry Bde started on a march into Suffolk for 4 days. Accompanied by our Section 1/2 3rd Fd. Ambulance under Capt. William R.A.M.C. in command. Ealing Med. Officer two was detailed from Cornwell's Clearing Station to accompany unit. Sick men were returned to bug'ds at Ipswich the motor ambulance, which was in readiness at the base where needed. The ammunition wagon for the march post close to Sanef Leet, from this acute men were felt or, opened. Em 1/6 + 1/4 Fans. Emb. Reg. Much grateful thankfulness was found. By the I.A. detachment as well as by the M.O.S. with other C.F.C. march.	
3-11-15	Monthly Conference about 1/2 Fans. Fd. Ambulance for Lucknow He showed an unsatisfactory state of things in the unit this unit has been unfortunate in losing laid in constant change of officers, due to the majority being been attached on Home Service. A fresh O.C. from numerous has now joined (Maj. Montenecury Smith) so there is hope for better things for the future in this respect.	E. Grubby. Lt.Col. R.A.M.C. O/C A.D.M.S. 3-12-15

Forms/C. 2118/10

Army Form C. 2118.

WAR DIARY
INTELLIGENCE SUMMARY.
(Erase heading not required.)

Hour, Date, Place	Summary of Events and Information	Remarks and references to Appendices
Harwich 6-11-15	Arrived with Norwich & Suffolk Hosp.¹ for attachment to Capt. Macpherson R.A.M.C. - O.C. Sn. on Harwich Garrison (temp.)	G.T.G
" 9-11-15	Arrived with M.O. ½s Cyclists at Trimley for the medical care of troops at Trim and Walton, to arrange for motor transport for Fd. Ars.	G.T.G
" 10-11-15	Direct direction from Central Force med. authorities, arranged for the institution of B.N.E. on men of all units in prevention of venereal diseases (includes venereal). This instruction to be given to all O.R.'s.	G.T.G
" 19-11-15	The incidence of (hard Chancre Sore) has been very small. Application made for treatment of sick from Divl. in Military Hosp. Ipswich, instead of sending them to Care Bridge. Authority from D.A.M.S. given.	G.T.G
" 25-11-15	Tactical Scheme. - Special scheme for R.A.M.C. — Medical unit to get quickly into touch with regimental aid posts & keep touch with regts. M.O.s during the operations, the scheme was in part proven when E.F.Y. (Remainder)	G.T.G
" 27-11-15	Leave on recommendation of Med. Board granted 6:Col. Herpens enrolled for 2 months from 17-11-15 (in internment)	G.T.G
" 30-11-15	Various Tactical Schemes have taken place during the month in which the R.A.M.C. units have taken part, & have furnished valuable information.	G. Kirshner Lt. Col. R.A.M.C A/c Div. 3-12-15

Army Form C. 2118.

WAR DIARY
or
INTELLIGENCE SUMMARY.
(Erase heading not required.)

Instructions regarding War Diaries and Intelligence Summaries are contained in F. S. Regs., Part II. and the Staff Manual respectively. Title pages will be prepared in manuscript.

Hour, Date, Place	Summary of Events and Information	Remarks and references to Appendices
2 Dec. — 1915	Inspection Cavalry Clearing Station in the field. Drills & ordinary movements done well. The necessity of intelligent knowledge of first aid work to personnel impressed in fine con[versation]	E.T.G
3 Dec. 1915	Arranged for treatment of Offs. N.C.os & men (8 Div) suffering from "frostbite", instead of sending them to 2 & 3 Fd. Hosps. Cambridge Mil. Hosp.	ETG
9 Dec. 1915	Divisional field day; all divisional units units engaged.	ETG
13 Dec. 1915	Discussion with A.P.M. concerning prevalence of venereal women in Ipswich. (High Bombard) A.P.M. acting in conjunction with civil police is cases where such is known.	ETG
15 Dec 1915	Lecture by Maj. Montgomery (Smith) specially for officers of medical service. Subject is — meat officers at their clubs in active service, and treating tuberculosis lecture.	ETG
17 Dec. 1915	A.F. C340 furnished to Hd. Qs., showing the deficiencies in the number of medical officers of the Division, pointing out the necessity of the recruit, the overheads regiment fill up vacancies.	GTG

[Stamp: 58th (LONDON) DIVISION GENERAL STAFF 2-JAN.1916]

E.T. Gubbins
COLONEL,
Assistant Director Medical Services,
58th (London) DIVISION.

WAR DIARY

INTELLIGENCE SUMMARY. A.D.M.S. 58 Lond. Div.

Army Form C. 2118.

(Erase heading not required.)

Instructions regarding War Diaries and Intelligence Summaries are contained in F.S. Regs., Part II. and the Staff Manual respectively. Title pages will be prepared in manuscript.

Hour, Date, Place	Summary of Events and Information	Remarks and references to Appendices
14-1-16 Ipswich	Instructions received for the preparation for mobilization of the 2/1, 2/2, 2/3 London Field Ambulances for service overseas. All the medical stores & the mobilization stores in possession use of old pattern, or if new service pattern, & regulations were immediately prepared for the necessary new materials. 15 Officers are needed & make up strength on approved for, the rest of the personnel is up to strength.	R.2. 927 14-1-16 [stamp: 58th (LONDON) DIVISION 5-FEB 1916 GENERAL STAFF] G.H.Q.
31-1-16 "	Mobilization of the three field ambulances is being completed; the medical stores are complete; but some of the personnel other than men Transport is still 6 men. There is still a deficiency of 15 Officers.	G.H.Q.

A.S. Cubbing Revnell
Lt. Col. A.D.M.S.
A/O 58 Lond. Div.

Army Form C. 2118.

WAR DIARY
or
INTELLIGENCE SUMMARY.
(Erase heading not required.)

Instructions regarding War Diaries and Intelligence Summaries are contained in F.S. Regs., Part II. and the Staff Manual respectively. Title pages will be prepared in manuscript.

Hour, Date, Place	Summary of Events and Information	Remarks and references to Appendices
21-2-16 Ipswich	2/1, 2/2, 2/3 City of London Field Ambulances with personnel complete, mobilization equipment complete (with the exception of 7 motor ambulances) receive orders to join the 56th Division. E.H.	[Stamp: 58th (LONDON DIVISION) 3-MAR.1916 GENERAL STAFF]
22-2-16 Ipswich	2/1, 2/2, 2/3 Home counties Field Ambulances arrived, with complete personel of N.C.O.s and men, mobilization equipment (except motor ambulances) but furnished with medical equipment. About 3 officers per unit required to complete. E.T.G.	

Ipswich
3-3-16

E.T. Gubbin
Col A.M.S
A.D.M.S.

Forms/C. 2118/10

www.ingramcontent.com/pod-product-compliance
Lightning Source LLC
Chambersburg PA
CBHW081515160426
43193CB00014B/2698